SHARKS!

PHONICS

Flatheads

Book 9: l-blends

By Qui

Photo Credits: cover: Fred Bavendam/Corbis; title page: [...] ages 4-5: Fred Bavendam/Corbis; pages 6-7: Carlos Villoch/Corbis; pages [...] en Frink/Corbis; pages 12-13: Stephen Frink /Getty Images; pages 14-[...] Stockphoto.

ISBN 978-0-545-74708-0

12 11 10 9 8 7 6 5 4 3 2 1   14 15 16 17 18/0

Printed in China   145

First Printing, September 2014

SCHOLASTIC INC.

What are these sharks called?

Here's a **clue**.

Look at their heads.

Do their heads look like a tool you know?

Their heads are wide and **flat**.
Their heads are short
and **blunt**.

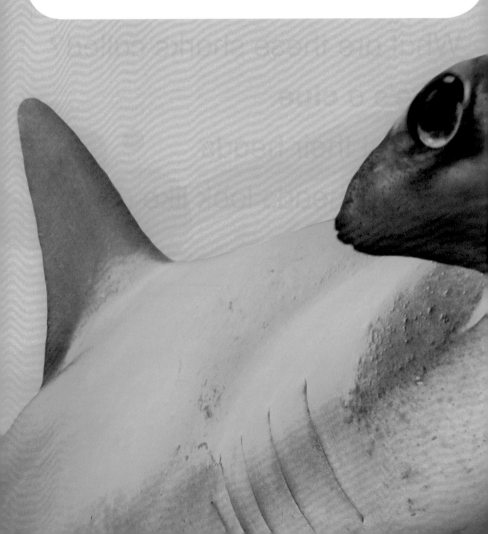

Their heads look like hammers!
They are called
hammerhead sharks.

The hammerheads' **flat** heads help them **slide** and **glide** through the water.

They **sling** their heads from side to side to look for prey.

These sharks spot something red, **blue**, and **sleek**.
Fish!

They **slide** their tails from side to side to **blast** through the water.

Some fish lie on the sand **floor** and try to **blend** in. But the hammerhead sharks don't need to see them. They smell them! They pin them in **place** with their **flat** heads and take a big bite.

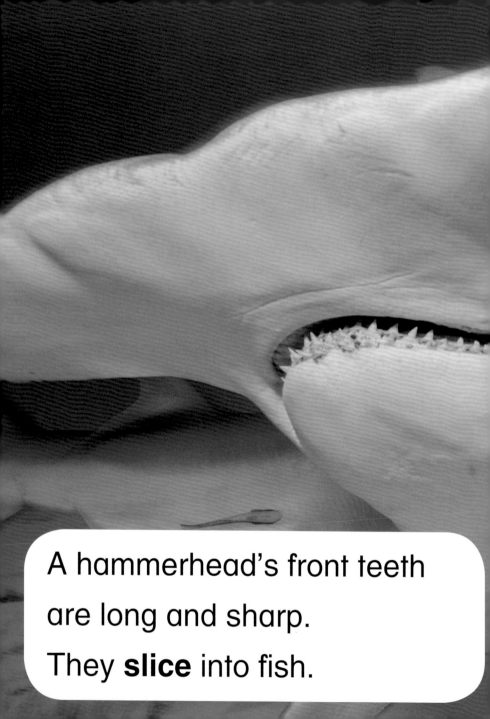

A hammerhead's front teeth are long and sharp.
They **slice** into fish.

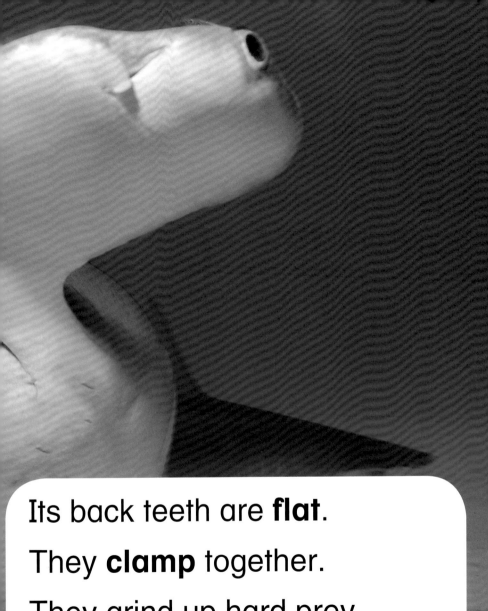

Its back teeth are **flat**.

They **clamp** together.

They grind up hard prey like crabs.

Hammerhead sharks are shy. They do not like to be **close** to people.

Stay **clear** if you see one.

They do not like to **play**.

Beware!

Hammerheads have **flat** heads and big bites!